More Than Just a Pretty Face

Queen Esther & Mordecai
The Dynamic Duo

TONI WRIGHT
AUTHOR

More Than Just a Pretty Face

Queen Esther & Mordecai
The Dynamic Duo

TONI WRIGHT
AUTHOR

Contact Info for more ordering:
Higher Ground Daily Inspirations
www.grace2wright.org

COPYRIGHT

More Than Just A Pretty Face

Copyright ©2021 by Toni Wright
First Edition, 2021

Front Cover by D/Keine

Inside Image by Moussa81

All rights reserved and printed in the United States of America. No part of this book may be used or reproduced, stored in a retrieval system, or transmitted, in any form or any manner by any means, electronic, mechanical, photocopying, recording, or otherwise, without prior written permission from the author.

For bulk purchases and special sales, please contact me through:

Higher Ground Daily Inspirations
www.grace2wright.org

Published in the United States of America. For Worldwide Distribution, Printed in the USA. All scripture versions used in this Book, otherwise indicated, are taken from The Thompson® Chain-Reference® Bible Fifth Improved Edition. Copyright ©2007 B.B. Kirkbride Bible Company, Inc. Indianapolis, Indiana USA 22nd Printing July 2018 King James Version (KJV). Copyright ©1908, 1917, 1929, 1934, 1957, 1964, 1982. 1988, By Frank Charles Thompson. All rights reserved worldwide. The English Standard Version ESV; New International Version (NIV).

TABLE OF CONTENTS

MORE THAN JUST A PRETTY FACE I

MORE THAN JUST A PRETTY FACE I

COPYRIGHT 1

TABLE OF CONTENTS 2

INTRODUCTION 1
    AND THE WINNER IS 1

DEDICATION 5

ACKNOWLEDGMENTS 1

BACKGROUND 6

CHAPTER ONE 1
    DRAMA AT THE PALACE 1

CHAPTER TWO 12
    THERE'S A NEW QUEEN ON THE BLOCK 12

CHAPTER THREE 19
HAMAN'S EVIL PLOT TO MASSACRE THE JEWS 19

CHAPTER FOUR 29
JEWS LAMENTATIONS 29

CHAPTER FIVE 36
ESTHER'S FIRST BANQUET 36

CHAPTER SIX 40
THE KING'S PLAN TO HONOR MORDECAI 40

CHAPTER SEVEN 47
QUEEN ESTHER REVEALS HER ADVERSARY 47

CHAPTER EIGHT 52
MORDECAI IS GIVEN 52

HAMAN'S WEALTH 52

CHAPTER NINE 60
HE ALWAYS CAUSES ME 60

TO TRIUMPH 60

CHAPTER TEN **70**

THE DYNAMIC DUO 70

ABOUT THE AUTHOR **74**

Dedication

This book is dedicated to my children, Desmond and wife Ava, to my daughter Mahogany, and my two grandchildren, Akiya and Jeremiah and to the rest of my beautiful family. Thank you for your support in this endeavor.

ACKNOWLEDGMENTS

I want to extend my deepest thanks to two extraordinary friends and consultants for their continued encouragement and support:

Debbie Bowie, educator, and businesswoman, for constantly critiquing, editing, and encouraging me to follow my heart. I appreciate your assistance and willingness to accompany me on this book-writing journey. Thank you for your insight, knowledge, and spiritual encouragement in making this possible. God bless you.

To Teresa Sweet, Businesswoman, and Associate. I sincerely appreciate your friendship, your daily words of encouragement, suggestions, and wisdom. God Bless you.

INTRODUCTION

AND THE WINNER IS

"And the winner is!" These are most likely the words heard at an actual modern-day beauty pageant. Some believe that beauty pageants are demeaning to women. In contrast, others believe that pageants are a way of celebrating a woman's beauty, talents, and abilities while still appreciating her more external features. A significant difference between the pageant of Esther's day and the pageant of today is that today's pageants are entirely voluntary. The contestants were not forced out of their homes to join the pageant. Another important fact is that today's contestants are paid a significant amount of money to participate. Anywhere from $25,000 to $250,000, scholarships, career opportunities, and prize packages." It is a billion-dollar industry, and the willing contestants have parents who spent thousands of dollars for their daughters to compete.

The pageant of Esther's day was the polar opposite. These young girls were most likely underage, brought in by the King's order, separated from their families and communities, rationed out food to keep them from gaining too much weight and control them. Harems came in a variety of shapes and sizes, and not all were created equal. Some harems in Persia housed royal women and the King's concubines who were held as slaves. I imagine the young girls were underage, and many were frightened of the men who took them captive. Even the keeper of the house was a man.

Terrified, unsuspecting, and intimidated, the young ladies were thrust into the era of their time and forced to grow up quickly. They had to adjust their mindset immediately if they wanted to survive this ordeal, yet some of them no doubt thought it might be exciting. Today, many people believe it was more like modern-day trafficking and believe it was an awful thing to do.

Esther participated in one of these so-called pageants, but it was because of Esther's God-given beauty that she was able to quickly find grace and favor with the king and secured her position as queen. Unsuspecting little Esther was more than just a pretty face. God blessed Esther with her beauty, and He used it for His glory. If Esther did not have the beauty she possessed, this would have been a different scenario, no doubt. But the King was looking for beauty, and Esther kept the King's requirements.

However, Esther's beauty was not only skin deep, but she also possessed God's inner beauty and fragrance. His grace and spirit also shined through and made Esther desirable. Everyone that looked upon her could not help but marvel at her beauty. Soon Esther would show the world that she was more than a pretty face as they waged battle against their enemies.

Esther was not only the winner of this "beauty pageant," but she was the Star of the story. Fortunately, while there were no runners-up in this story and no first or second place, others played an integral part and were winners. You will see them as you travel through this book's chapters because Esther was generous in sharing the spotlight. She possessed genuine leadership qualities, and as a result, true deliverance came to her people.

Esther was humble yet confident, unassuming yet courageous, self-sacrificing yet bold enough to demand the heads of her adversaries. The Book of Esther is not only a lesson in God's providence, protection, and grace, but it also contains several nuggets that we can carry with us on our journey through life.

The book tells us that God uses whomever He chooses and makes no apologies for it. When setting forth His will, He defies all traditional ideas of who He allows doing what and who He does not allow. God is unconstrained by man's prejudices and expectations of what He will enable. We belong to Him, and He works everything out after the counsel of His will. (Ephesians 1:11)

"O the depth of the riches of the wisdom and knowledge of God! How unsearchable are his judgments and his ways past finding out! For whom hath known the mind of the Lord? Or who hath been his counselor?" Romans 11:33-34

The story shows how God arranged the events and facts surrounding His chosen people amid the audacious schemes the enemy devised to wipe them off the face of the earth. God is keeping His hidden weapon in plain sight, as we can see. He can do so because man believes he is more intelligent than God. The enemy is defeated thanks to the foresight and strategy of these two unwitting individuals. Who would have guessed that a little orphan girl raised by her (heroic) cousin would be the savior of this great people?

While there is more than one winner in our story, there is only one chosen Star. Her birth name is Hadassah (meaning Myrtle, a plant associated with love, peace, fertility, and youth.) Hadassah's name was later changed to Esther by Mordecai, Esther's cousin, when she was carried away to Persia. Esther (meaning Star, in Persia). How appropriate is the meaning of her name, for she was indeed the Star of this story?

ESTHER AFFIRMATIONS

I Am A Queen Chosen By God

I Am A Royal Priesthood

I Am A Woman Of God

I Am Who God Says I Am

I Am Unique

I Am Wondrously Made By God

I Am Blessed And Highly Favored

I Am More Than A Conqueror

I Am A True Worshipper

I Am A Model For Leadership

I Am Used Of God

I Am The Apple Of His Eye

I Am Bold and Courageous

BACKGROUND

The Book of Esther takes place in the third year of King Ahasuerus, that is, Xerxes I. While some scholars believe Mordecai wrote the Book of Esther, no evidence of authorship exists.

Esther's story reads like a dramatic Hollywood movie, with a storyline based on "Rags to Riches" and several films based on the Book of Esther. I can see why Hollywood would make a movie based on the Book of Esther because it incorporates all the elements present in our current-day movies. Some of those elements include lies, jealousy, anger, racism, greed, inequality, attempted political assassinations, pride, hate, abuse of power, drunkenness, and murder. From a global perspective, more and more films with these elements are becoming increasingly popular.

Hadassah (Esther's Hebrew name from birth) lost both of her parents at a young age, and by God's providence, Mordecai, Hadassah's cousin, was right there to take on the enormous burden of raising a child. Esther and Mordecai were taken away to Susa, the citadel, as young Hadassah grew older. Hegai oversaw Hadassah when she was taken to the House of Women. Mordecai warned Hadassah not to reveal her identity, so Hadassah changed her name to Esther, the Persian version (meaning Star).

Some people see a glass as half-full, while others see it as half-empty. At the house of women, I am sure that taught young Hadassah how to care for her body and personal needs that only a mother or a woman can teach another woman. Even though Hegai was a male, some women taught younger women about their bodies. Once again, God's providence is at work.

Isaiah 61:3, "To appoint unto them that mourn in Zion, to give unto them beauty for ashes, the oil of joy for mourning, the garment of praise for the spirit of heaviness; that they might be called trees of righteousness, the planting of the LORD, that he might be glorified." God is not oblivious to our past tragedies and suffering, and he was conscious of Esther's ordeal as a child. That is how God works: He takes something that was supposed to destroy us and turns it into something beautiful. *Romans 8:28 – "And we know that all things work together for good to them that love God, to them who are the called according to his purpose."* You can tell a lot from someone's testimony. Listen to what Mary says in *Luke 1:48, "For he hath regarded the low estate of his handmaiden: for, behold, from henceforth all generations shall call me blessed."* There is always a story behind your glory, and if you listen closely to the testimonies in the Bible, it is no different. God rewards us when we hold to His hand, His unchanging hand, because He will see us through.

Little did Esther know that God's all-seeing eye saw everything that she had gone through as she was growing up. While Mordecai did an excellent job raising Esther, nothing compares with growing up with a good mother to confide in girl stuff. God knew how great the ache in Esther's heart was and what she must have felt growing up as a little girl every day. God said, *"I'll exchange your sorrow and give you great joy, beauty for your ashes."* He fulfilled His promise to Esther and showed her His faithfulness. If you hold on to God and be patient, He will give you beauty for your ashes and the desires of your heart.

Your background, where you were born, who your parents

were, and your education does not define who you are as a person, nor does it dictate your future unless you allow it to. You can dream as big as you dare to believe and know that nothing is too hard for God to perform in your life. *Mark 10:27 "...with man, it is impossible, but not with God. For all things are possible with God."*

Keep your eyes on God as you go through the storms and challenges of life, and like a Father, He will gently guide you to your destination. He is always there, working in the shadows and devising each detail of your life. It may not always look like it, but He has promised you, *"...I will never leave you, nor forsake you." Hebrews 13:5.* God oversees the affairs of humanity and the affairs of His chosen people, you. His providence is ever-present; no matter what you are going through or what you have been through, Jesus says, *"...I am the Alfa and Omega, the beginning, and the end..." Revelations 1:8, 21:6, and 22:13,* and *"He is the author and the finisher of your faith."* God finishes what He starts, and He will be with you to the end. Nothing can pluck you out of His hand.

The Book of Esther and the Book of Ruth may be the only two books of the Bible coined after a woman, but it is by far not the only two stories in the Bible of how God used women to fulfill His purpose. Look around you today; God is still using women to do great things. We have a woman serving as the Vice President of the United States. Four women commanders of warships, and the list goes on. *"What shall we then say to these things? If God be for us, who can be against us?" Romans 8:31.*

CHAPTER ONE

DRAMA AT THE PALACE

The Book of Esther is set in the third year of the reign of king Ahasuerus. This climatic story begins with the king throwing himself an extravagant banquet that lasted close to six months (180 days) and given in two parts. The king wanted to show off all his magnificent wealth, riches, majesty, and royal estate. Besides that, he wanted to "flaunt" his wife's beauty before his guest. Some say it was a military move because they were about to go to war with Greece. The first banquet consisted of his military leaders, nobles, the highest-ranking officials, dignitaries, and the princes over his kingdom. His kingdom extended from India to Ethiopia, which spanned more than one hundred and twenty-seven provinces. For one hundred and eighty days, they enjoyed the king's hospitality, entertainment, wealth, and war talks. King Ahasuerus was one of the world's wealthiest individuals. (1:4)

The second banquet, which immediately followed, lasted seven days and was equally magnificent. The entire population of Shushan's palace was invited; those of high and low status alike. This banquet was held in the court of the garden of the king's palace. Can you imagine how exciting this must have been for ordinary people? For seven days, everyone had the opportunity to experience how the rich and famous partied. Furthermore, they could eat extravagant food that they could never afford independently and had likely never heard of before. Currently, it would be like being invited to the Parliament of the British Royal Family.

The vessels they drank from were made of diverse shades of gold, and the walls were made of marble. The beds were made of gold and silver and laid on red, blue, white, and black marble pavements. The drapes were blue and fastened with cords of fine linens of purple with silver rings, pillars of marble, and mother-of-pearl, and precious stones. It was a banquet to die for, especially for the everyday folks who have never experienced such an event. They drank the best wine, royal wine, and could drink until their heart's desire. They could drink themselves to oblivion, as the king had ordered, and no one could stop them. There were no restrictions on how much alcohol they consumed. This was the atmosphere, and there were no boundaries set except to disobey the king. (Esther 1:7-8).

Vashti, King Ahasuerus' Queen, hosted a feast for the women in the royal house. (The house belonged to the king, and it is a strong probability the women belonged to the king as well.) As the ladies were drinking their wine, there came a knock at the door from the king's seven eunuchs Mehuman, Biztha, Harbona, Bigtha, Abagtha, Zethar, and Carcas, ordering Queen Vashti's presence at the banquet. I can imagine it went something like this, "Queen Vashti, the king commands your presence before the court. He has commanded that you come wearing only your crown." If looks could kill! Vashti answers, "Say what?" I can imagine that was not the only thing Vashti said, and she may also have had a few choice words for them, one being "NO!" Vashti sent the eunuchs running back to the king with a resounding, "No."

The answer sent shockwaves through the King's body, no doubt. It was not the reaction, let alone a response that the king had expected. Had Vashti lost her mind? Could she have been inebriated? The king could not accept Vashti's defiant behavior, especially in front of the guest. It made him look highly insignificant in the eyes of the people, especially his men. Vashti's response did not project the king as a powerful ruler over one-hundred and twenty-seven provinces but a king who had no control or influence over his woman. He was humiliated, and he had to do something about it quickly.

We are not sure why Vashti chose not to obey the king at this time, maybe she had too much to drink, or perhaps she did not have enough to drink! But Vashti did not want to be subjected to the whims of a drunken king and his soldiers. So, Vashti sent all seven of the king's chamberlains Mehuman, Biztha, Harbona, Bigtha, Abagtha, Zethar, and Carcas, running back to the king with her bold, outspoken reply, "No! Not tonight! I have a headache!"

When the king got word, he was furious. The Bible says, *"A soft answer turns away wrath: but grievous words stir up anger." Proverbs 15:1.* Sometimes a soft answer turns away wrath, but I do not think it would have mattered much in this case. However, Vashti's response would alter the course of her life (the one she was accustomed to) and the kingdom. As the king's anger burned within him, he sought advice from his counselors.

CONVERSATIONAL THOUGHT

Was it pride, alcohol, or just downright rebellion? Maybe it was a glimpse of the first "Me Too" movement. Whatever it was, one thing we know is that it was God's will and God's timing for a new queen (Esther) to take the throne. But there are always nuggets throughout scripture for us to learn. How would you explain the implications behind Vashti's behavior? Is there a time to disobey those who are in authority when it comes to your sexuality?

Unfortunately, the king considered these women to be his personal property rather than members of the royal family. Maybe she had enough, and the humiliation and shame she had suffered as a result of the king's inebriated order would result in a greater disgrace than the consequences she'd face otherwise. We will never actually know the answer. **"You are the only one that can put a price on your self-worth."**

Did Vashti not know she was the king's property or did she no longer care? She was his prize, and he could command her to do as he pleased (so he thought). Vashti's response dealt a crushing blow to the king's ego. Regardless, she paid a hefty price for disobeying the king's inebriated command.

It's Complicated

I am sure the king was thinking, "how dare she embarrass and disrespect me? I am the king. Who does she think she is?" The ego got a little bruised that evening, and the king was furious. The king conferred with his advisors on the appropriate punishment for Vashti. He simply could not let her get away with disrespecting him. Her actions had to be dealt with immediately. The seven princes of Persia and Media, with whom he consulted, knew they had better do something quick. "*It is interesting to note that the king did not take matters into his own hand regarding Vashti, but he sought legal advice from counsel. He listened and followed their advice. Some leaders refuse to listen to anybody and are quick to point the finger at others when things do not go their way.*

The king's wise men debated the issue, and Memucan stepped forward to respond to the king. He rebuked Vashti's behavior for being defiant and decided that she deserved harsh punishment. Why the urgency? They assumed Vashti's actions would persuade other women to follow in her footsteps. Furthermore, they did not want the king to appear weak in front of his subjects, so he had to deal with Vashti right away. According to the king's legal team, Vashti's conduct would defeat men's leadership in the home and wives. If Vashti got away with disobeying the King, men would be disrespected and hated by their wives. In the Kingdom, this was no small matter ("because men ruled!"). The men were big on that.

Conversational Thought

The bottom line is, God chose Esther, and Vashti's time was up. That did not mean that God put Vashti up to say no; she had probably had enough of being humiliated. We do not know, but given the circumstances, it is highly probable. But there are still lessons we can learn from Vashti's defiant behavior to the king. Many women (and some men) feel they must accommodate or compromise their beliefs and values because of the perpetrator's position. But, just like Vashti, you have a choice. Consider what Vashti gave up; it might have even been her life. It seems that there are occasions when you should be outspoken or aggressive in your reaction to unwelcome advances that compromise your values.

- Vashti refused to obey the king when her culture demanded complete submission to the king. How can you explain to a young lady that she has a choice not to compromise her moral values regardless of who is putting pressure on her?
- Peer pressure is a relentless force in the lives of young people. Young people must realize that standing up for their convictions and saying "no" will not always make them popular with their peers.

Ashamed and Broken

I am sure everyone was talking about the drama at the banquet.

What happened to Vashti was on the lips of every woman in attendance, how she dared to reject the king's command. Some women may not have agreed with Vashti's disobedience, while others secretly admired her and wished they had the courage to follow in her footsteps. For this reason, the king's counsel advised that the king issue an unchangeable royal commandment in the Persian and Medes' law, that Vashti can never again come before the king and allow someone better than she to inherit her royal estate. Vashti had to understand that her defiance would have dire consequences. She must have believed that whatever principles she based her decision on meant more to her than compromising those principles. On the other hand, maybe she does not even know why she said "No."

The decree was published among all one-hundred and twenty-seven provinces that all wives shall give their husbands honor, both great and small (regardless of their positions). Obey and serve or suffer the consequences. Vashti was deposed, shamed, and dethroned.

FREE WILL (CONVERSATIONAL THOUGHT)

We know it was God's will for Esther to be Queen, but God does not cause people to do evil, but He does use evil for His own good. God is in the business of carrying out His plans and His will. He uses good and evil for His purpose.

James 1:13 reminds us, "Let no man say when he is tempted, I am tempted of God: for God cannot be tempted with evil, neither (does he tempt) any man (with evil)."

All of us have the freedom of choice and free will to do what we want to do. That is God's gift to us.

THE PRIDE OF LIFE

What started all this drama in the first place? It was the pride of life and man's choice to exercise his right to live the way as he pleases. Pride causes abuse of power and poor judgment. Pride and alcohol fuel abuse in many cases and is a terrible combination. Many prophets, including Paul, warned against being intoxicated as well as Proverbs.

Proverbs 20:1 says, "Wine is a mocker, strong drink is raging, and whosoever is deceived thereby is not wise."

Ephesians 5:18 "And be not drunk with wine, wherein is excess, but be filled with the Spirit."

The Bible is clear when speaking about being in a drunken stupor. This is not so much a criticism of alcohol as it is of being a drunkard.

PRIDE'S DESTRUCTION

"A man's pride shall bring him low: but honor shall uphold the humble in spirit." (Proverbs 29:23) Many places in scripture illustrate how pride brought great men down and is still doing so today. Pride is what brought Pharaoh down in the Book of Exodus 15:4, Sennacherib in II Chronicles 32:21, Nebuchadnezzar in the Book of Daniel 4:33, and many other places in the Bible. Pride is

what got Satan kicked out of heaven. The Bible is not the only place we can look to see the devastation of pride's destructive outcome. All we must do is turn on the news or the investigative channel, and we will see pride's raw destructive nature playing out in the lives of sometimes unsuspecting and innocent people.

THE KING'S MANDATE

"And when the king's decree which he shall make shall be published throughout all his empire, (for it is great) all the wives shall give to their husbands' honor, both to great and small." "...that every man should bear rule in his own house, and that it should be published according to the language of every people." (21-22). The message the king sent out was explicitly addressed to the women of the kingdom. The letter was sent in all languages so there would be no confusion. The king believed that men should rule their own houses. The New Testament is analogous by nature but significantly more profound in context and direction.

1 Timothy 3:2-5 "A bishop then must be blameless, the husband of one wife, vigilant, sober, of good behavior, given to hospitality, apt to teach: Not given to wine (drunkard), ... One that (rules) well his own house, ...For if a man knows not how to rule his own house, how shall he take care of the church of God?"

While this scripture addresses Bishops, it also serves as a model for all Christian men not to be drunkards, and not be an adulterer, and be an example to other Christian men. However, the king was all the above, and was prone to drunkenness, had no regard for his first wife, and was willing to kill people he did not even know.

It Is Time to Go to The Next Level

There is no indication that the prospect of becoming Queen burdened Esther. Esther's upbringing by Mordecai may have prepared her to deal with a powerful personality like the king. Even though Mordecai did not serve as a leader, he possessed leadership qualities and quickly rose to prominence as a leader. He refused to bow to Haman, his adversary, and the story continues to show several defining moments of leadership in Mordecai's life. Mordecai raised Esther and taught her everything she knew from when she was a child until she was taken away to the palace. Mordecai visited Esther every day after she arrived at the house of women.

Mordecai was a role model for Esther, which explains why Esther was able to make such bold decisions in the face of adversity. Mordecai had a commanding personality, which Esther most likely inherited. Esther is the protagonist of this novel, but she did not act alone. Esther is a team player, so she was able to bring deliverance to the people. Her relationship with Mordecai would play a crucial role in her relationship with the king. God was always in Esther's life, orchestrating the events of her life and bringing her to this defining moment.

God Chooses Whom He Would

God is concerned about His people and purpose. Galatians 3:28 *"There is neither Jew nor Greek, there is neither bond nor free, there is neither male nor female: for ye are all one in Christ Jesus."* We are all equal in Christ. No one is superior to the other. Jews are not superior to Greeks, free people are not superior to slaves, men are not superior to women, and no race is superior to the other.

It is a fact that God chose Esther for His purpose, and we must also remember that God chose Mordecai to raise Esther. **God purposely brings people into our lives to help us grow into the person He wants us to become.** *Proverbs 11:6 says, "Train up a child in the way he should go: and when he is old, he will not depart from it."*

Conversational Thought

Recently, I read an article in Psychology Today written by Jen Kromberg PsyD, which suggests that "if there was a dad or other male caregiver early in one's childhood, he probably set the first model of how a relationship with a man should be...for better or for worse." (Jen Kromberg PsyD How Dads Shape Daughters' Relationships).

CHAPTER TWO

THERE'S A NEW QUEEN ON THE BLOCK

"*The blessing of the Lord is in the reward of the godly, and suddenly he maketh his blessing to flourish."* (Ecclesiastes 11:22)

The Bible says, *"after these things, when the wrath of king Ahasuerus was appeased, he remembered Vashti, and what she had done, and what was decreed against her."* (2:1). When the king was sober again, the king began to recall the night's events with Vashti. The king started to miss Vashti, and his servants ministered to him and suggested the king search for a new bride. (**Note:** Some believe there was a four-year gap between Chapter One and Chapter Two.

THE SEARCH FOR THE NEW QUEEN

The preparations for the search to find the king a new queen began. The young virgins were gathered in the palace and given purification products. Esther did not need as many beauty products as the other girls, so Hegai gave Esther only what she needed.

Mordecai, the son of Jair, the son of Shimei, the son of Kish, a Benjamite, had been carried away from Jerusalem with the captivity of Jeconiah king of Judah, whom Nebuchadnezzar the king of Babylon carried away captive. Mordecai sat at the gate at Shushan the palace. He had brought Hadassah (now called Esther) with him to the palace and warned her not to reveal her identity, so she changed her name from Hadassah to Esther. Hadassah was a Hebrew name meaning "Myrtle" (a plant associated with love, peace, fertility, and youth)." Esther (meaning "Star, Myrtle, Bride"), a Persian equivalent to Hadassah. The name Hadassah also signifies innocence, purity, hope, love, and compassion.

BLESSED AND HIGHLY FAVOURED

"And the angel came in unto her, and said, Hail, thou that art highly favored, the Lord is with thee: blessed art thou among women." Luke 1:28. The maidens and young Esther were gathered and brought to Hagai, the Housekeeper of the women. From the moment the young ladies entered the palace until Esther received the crown for Queen, Esther's life quickly unfolded over the next two years. Esther immediately won the king's favor; from the moment he saw her, he loved her. Her beauty was a contributing factor of God's external blessings on her life, but she also possessed God's inner beauty and grace. That is why when the king saw Esther, he was immediately smitten by her beauty. (v 9) The search was over. He fell in love

with her (according to scripture). Esther found favor with everyone that looked upon her.

Vashti was beautiful as well, but God's favor and blessings enhanced Esther's beauty. Thus, goes the saying, "beauty is only skin deep." *"Charm is deceitful, and beauty is passing, but a woman who fears the Lord, she shall be praised." Proverbs 31:30.* I am sure Mordecai must have taught Esther these values down through the years.

BLESSED AND FAVOURED

When it comes to God's blessings on your life and the trials you face, external forces have no bearing on your worth. Take, for instance, Mary. The angel Gabrielle greeted Mary with the words, *"Hail, thou that art highly favored, the Lord is with thee: blessed art thou among women." Luke 1:28.* When the angel brought those greetings to Mary, Mary was unknown and had no known worldly value other than her engagement to Joseph. In fact, in her song of praises to the Lord, Mary says, *"For he has regarded the low state of His maidservant; For henceforth all generations shall call me blessed." Luke 1:48 (NKJV).* Mary's testimony to Elisabeth tells you a little about how she felt. She said, "I am a nobody (unknown), but YOU have made me somebody." Esther, who was orphaned at a young age and raised by a foster parent, was also an unknown but made a queen by God. It did not look like she was blessed and highly favored either. In other words, their lives had not reflected the "favor" the world considers as "blessed." Each female was highly favored of the Lord, but not by man's viewpoint. Be careful how you judge those that may not have the same opportunities or blessings you may consider "blessed."

Moreover, these women had nothing to do with the favor on their lives. It was a gift from God. *Psalms 5:12 says, "For you bless the righteous, O Lord; you cover him with favor as with a shield."*

You are blessed and highly favored, and it has nothing to do with how smart you are, who your parents are, your background, how many people you know, or your economic or educational status. When you consider your purpose or your struggle, think about who might be tied to your struggle. Could your suffering be connected to someone else? To bring about deliverance in someone else's life, perhaps? Maybe your suffering is linked to generations to come? Esther's whole life had prepared her for this moment and time in her life. Her childhood trauma, unbeknownst to her, was tied to the deliverance of the Jewish people. She did not allow negative thoughts, people, or her past to cause bitterness into her heart.

Nobody knew that this little unknown, unassuming, hiding in plain sight young girl would one day become the queen of a nation. They never saw it coming, and that is the way God wants it. *Ephesians 3:20 says that "God can do exceedingly abundantly above all we can ask or think."* Never underestimate those around you based on outward appearances and external accomplishments. *"But the Lord said unto Samuel, Look not on his countenance, or on the height of his stature; because I have refused him: for the Lord seeth not as man seeth; for man looketh on the outward appearance, but the Lord looketh on the heart." 1 Samuel 16:7.*

If your time has not come yet, stay the course, it is on the way. God sees the big picture. He sees what you cannot see and holds the future in his hands. Nothing takes Him by surprise or away from his purpose. You do not have to try to impress anyone to get them to see that God is in your life. You are not alone, ever. He has promised never to forsake you. You are the apple of His eye. You do not have to hate on someone else to get ahead; the Bible says, *"Lift not up your horn on high: speak not with a stiff neck. For promotion cometh neither from the east, nor from the west, nor from the south. But God is the judge: he putteth down one, and setteth up another." Psalms 75:5-7.* God causes the rain to fall and the sun to shine in our lives.

What God has for you is for you, and nobody else can take it away from you and be successful. God's time for Esther had come, and she did not have to step on anyone to possess it. Yes, it was a blessing for Esther to be Queen, or we would not be reading about her today. The Bible declares, *"He will arise and have mercy on Zion; For the time to favour her, yea, the set time, is come." Psalms 102:13.* God has designated a set time to bless you and perform his purpose and will in your life. *"For surely there is an end (to that thing you have been praying about), and your expectation (hope, belief) shall not be cut off (disappointing). Hear thou, my son, and be wise, and guide thine heart in the way." Proverbs 23:18-19.*

THE PLOT AGAINST THE KING REVEALED

IF YOU SEE SOMETHING, SAY SOMETHING

"For they intended evil against thee: they imagined a mischievous device, which they are not able to perform." Psalms 21:11. One day while Mordecai was at work sitting at the king's gate, he overheard two of the king's chamberlains, Bigthan and Teresh, plotting to kill the king. Mordecai revealed it to the queen, and the queen revealed it to the king. After verifying the plot, the king ordered the two to hang. The foiled scheme was published in the Book of Chronicles before the king, revealing that Mordecai exposed the plot. Sometimes when you do what is right, it may not always seem like a big deal, but the Bible says, *"God is not unrighteous to forget your work and labor of love..." Hebrews 6:10.* Even if your good deeds do not seem to be important to you, God remembers them. You may not see the rewards in your life right away, but God sees and never forgets your righteous acts of kindness.

Mordecai was in the right place at the right time and did the right thing. To "see something or hear something, then do something" requires a solid, morally inclined person. People are so afraid of retaliation or fearful of going against the crowd that they keep quiet. They say, "I don't want to get involved, or it's none of my business." But, as the saying goes, *"if you see something, say something, especially if it is going to save someone's life!"* You may or may not get a reward from man, but your reward will come from the Greatest rewarder of all, God. Mordecai did not allow fear to stop him because he put his trust in God. Mordecai did not pursue accolades for doing what was right.

Psalms 27:2-3, "When the wicked, even mine enemies and my foes, came upon me to eat up my flesh, they stumbled and fell. Though an army may encamp against me, My heart shall not fear; Though war may rise against me, in this I will be confident."

CHAPTER THREE

HAMAN'S EVIL PLOT TO MASSACRE THE JEWS

Under King Ahasuerus, Haman, the king's vizier and the son of Hammedatha the Agagite, was promoted to the second seat, above all the king's servants and princes. The king ordered all his servants to bow before Haman. However, Mordecai refused to bow before Haman despite the king's orders. When the king's servants saw Mordecai refusing to bow to Haman, they went to him every day and questioned him about it, hoping to elicit an answer. Mordecai finally admitted that it was because he was a Jew. The men were going to Haman to tell him what Mordecai had said to see how the situation would play out. Haman was so angry that he thought about killing Mordecai at that moment but instead devised a plan to wipe out all Jews from the face of the earth. Haman's hatred against Jews stemmed from God's order to Saul to exterminate all Agagites.

1 Samuel the 15:2 "Thus saith the LORD of hosts, "I remember that which Amalek did to Israel, how he waited for him in the way, when he came up from Egypt. Now go and smite Amalek, and destroy all that they have, and spare them not; but slay both man and woman, infant and suckling, oxen and sheep, camel and ass."

Unfortunately, Saul disobeyed God, and Samuel was forced to carry out God's will by assassinating the Agagite king. *"Thy sword hath made women childless, so shall thy mother be childless among women. And Samuel hewed Agag in pieces before the Lord in Gilgal."*

So, aside from Mordecai's reluctance to bow, there is some tradition behind Haman's anti-Semitism. In the Abrahamic law, the ten commandments' states, *"Thou shalt have no other god besides me." (Exodus 20:2 and again in Deuteronomy 5:6, and in Exodus 20:5 we are told, "Thou shalt not bow down thyself to them, nor serve them: for I, the LORD thy God am a jealous God."* Bowing to man was considered idolatry and punishable by death. Mordecai understood the law in this regard. Maybe that is why Haman said, *"they have their own laws; they are rebellious, and they are not obligated to obey the laws here. Therefore, they are unprofitable and should be destroyed."*

How Do You Respond To Your Enemy's Promotion?

Haman was promoted, although God knew his intentions to

massacre the Jews. Sometimes our enemies still seem to get blessed and seem to get away with murder (sort-of-speak). "How do you react when your enemy gets a promotion, or when something good happens to them after they did you wrong?" This is an issue that many people face. We see it all the time in our jobs, in the government, in systemic racism, even when your spouse walks off and leaves you with all the children. How do you respond when the perpetrators seem to keep getting "blessed," and you are left with a burden? How does it make you feel when it looks like evil is in control?

David had something to say about how this made him feel. He said: *Psalms 73:2-6 reads, "But as for me, my feet were almost gone; my steps had well-nigh slipped. For I was envious at the foolish when I saw the prosperity of the wicked. They are not in trouble as other men. Therefore, pride compasses them about as a chain; violence covereth them as a garment."* David goes on to say:

Psalms 37:35, "I have seen the wicked in great power, and spreading himself like a green bay tree. Yet he passed away, and, lo, he was not: yea, I sought him, but he could not be found." (36)

On the other hand, David gained new insight and revelation on the situation when he "went into the presence of the LORD or went to Church." He realized he had not considered the whole truth of the matter. Much like some of us who feel like the wicked are in great power and everything they do prosper (that they get away with it). David said, "I looked up, and they were gone; they had passed away. I could not find them anymore."

It is easy to become angry and bitter when there seems to be so little justice, and chaos is happening globally. The Jewish people were being targeted because of one man who hated them and made others feel the same way. They were targeted because of their race and the history behind the Jews and Haman's ancestors. Plain and simple, it was racism with a twist. God was with the Jews and would only allow this evil to reign for only so long. But that is not the way it looked. It is easy to blame God when it seems like you are not getting the justice you feel you deserve. But we must be careful not to allow bitterness to creep into our hearts. We must be careful not to turn our hearts away from God amid the confusion and turmoil we see and are experiencing in the world. David said, *"I almost let go of his hand, I almost slipped and fell out of fellowship with God, but God understood, and he held on to me."* God has promised, He will never leave you, nor forsake you. Nothing is a surprise to God. He is El Roi, *"the God who sees me." Hagar named the place where she was, El Roi in the Book of Genesis, "And she called the name of the Lord that spake unto her, Thou God seest me: for she said, Have I also here looked after him that seeth me?" Genesis 16:13.* God sees you, and He knows what you are going through.

"Do not avenge yourselves, beloved, but leave room for God's wrath. For it is written: "Vengeance is Mine; I will repay, says the Lord." Romans 12:19.

You do not have to be envious of the wicked or think that God does not see what is happening to you and the world. Read these scriptures for comfort and strength. *Psalms, 34, 35, 37, and 73.* These scriptures are very encouraging, and I must admit, I must go into my spiritual sanctuary and read them myself for hope and encouragement. Hopefully, they will help you to understand and get you through the hard times, as well.

The Book of Esther is not only about God's extraordinary providence, for which we are eternally grateful to God. But there are so many nuggets in the book that will give our hearts something to ponder over. The Jewish people were about to face one of the most challenging trials of their life instigated by a tyrant. He was bad enough when he held the position as the king's officer, but now he had an even more influential role. He was the second most powerful man in the kingdom. While we do not take the enemy's place in the world lightly, "the bigger they are, the harder they fall." Ask some of the most powerful men who were brought down just in the last ten years.

But the battle is not yours alone. *II Chronicles 20:15 says, "...the battle is not yours but God's."* You are in a fight against good and evil, and the winner is God. You already know who the winner is, and that must be your focus. It is not over until God says it is over. You must have some unique scriptures that will speak to your situation, pick you up and encourage you during those difficult times. If someone is fighting against you), they might find themselves fighting against God. *"But if it is from God, you will not be able to stop them. You may even find yourselves fighting against God." Acts 5:39.* The Great Jehovah was with Esther, and He knew what was coming down the pike against His people. They were not alone, and with Esther becoming Queen, there was no way evil would win.

EVIL PROMOTED

Haman was an egotistical, maniacal, narcissistic, and conniving person. But he was also very much liked by the king and promoted to a very prestigious position. In fact, some dictionaries say his name means "the magnificent, illustrious" well, we know he thought he was, and he thought very highly of himself. The king commanded that all his princes and everyone under him bow before Haman and show him reverence.

Since Mordecai refused to bow before him and not only refused to bow but also refused to move as Haman passed by, Haman's anger grew even more potent. He resolved within himself to assassinate Mordecai and exterminate the Jewish people. As a result, Haman set his evil plot against the Jews in motion.

THE PLOT

In the first month, that is, the month Nisan, in the twelfth year of king Ahasuerus, they cast Pur, that is, the lot, before Haman from day to day, and from month to month, to the twelfth month, that is, the month of Adar (March). (8) And Haman said unto king Ahasuerus, There is a certain people scattered abroad and dispersed among the people in all the provinces of thy kingdom, and their laws are diverse from all people; neither keep they the king's laws: therefore, it is not for the king's profit to suffer them. If it pleases the king, let it be written that they may be destroyed: and I will pay ten thousand talents of silver to the hands of those that have the charge of the business, to bring it into the king's treasuries. (Esther 3:7-8)

THE WICKED IS ALWAYS PLOTTING

The Bible says, *"The wicked plotteth against the just, and gnashes upon him with his teeth. The LORD shall laugh at him: for He seeth that his day is coming." Psalms 37:12*

When your adversary plots to kill you or strip away your rights, God is not surprised. That is when you would oppose him on every end. *"Fret not thyself because of evildoers, neither be thou envious against the workers of iniquity. For they shall soon be cut down like the grass and wither as the green herb."* There will always be those who plot to harm the innocent or the most vulnerable. It is a never-ending war, but like the Jews, you cannot give up and surrender. The adversary wishes for people to lose their salvation. "Fight the good fight of faith," the Bible says. Mordecai was a strong-willed man who was not afraid to stand up to evil. Mordecai believed that *"No weapon formed against "me" shall prosper, and every tongue that shall rise against "me" in judgment I "thou" shalt condemn: This is the heritage of the servants of the LORD, and their righteousness is of me, saith the LORD." Isaiah 54:17.*

Your Fight Is Not With Man

The Bible tells us, *"For we wrestle not against flesh and blood, but against principalities, against powers, against the rulers of the darkness of this world, against spiritual wickedness in high places. Ephesians 6:20.* We are often angered by those who commit crimes against humanity and condemn them, but we are not fighting man; we are fighting supernatural wickedness in high places. They are aware of who they are.

Vengeance Is Not Yours

"...Haman sought to destroy all the Jews that were throughout the whole kingdom of Ahasuerus, even the people of Mordecai." (Esther 3:6) Haman's hatred of the Jewish people went back as far as Exodus 17:8-16 and Deuteronomy 25:17-19.

When the king learned that there were people who would not abide by the laws of the Persians, Haman knew he would incite the king's wrath and provoke him to go along with his evil plan. He started his cruel ruse to carry out the scheme once he had the king's approval.

BEHOLD ALL SOULS ARE MINE

"Behold, all souls are mine; as the soul of the father, so also the soul of the son is mine: the soul that sinneth, it shall die." Ezekiel 18:4. All lives matter to God because He is the creator of all life. He created man in His image and likeness. So says the scripture. *Genesis 1:27* says, *"So, God created man (humanity) in his own image, in the image of God created he him."* Piper writes, "Man was created to be a graphic image of the Creator - a formal, visible representation of who God is and what God is."

Simply put, "people of every race deserve equal dignity and equal rights under the law." Who is he who would be so bold as to take even one of God's least ones or kill a man as if you created that life? With man, you might get away with it, but God sees all and is the ultimate judge. He said, *"vengeance is mine, and I will repay." Romans 12:19.*

PUBLICATION OF THE DECREE

"And the king took his ring from his hand, and gave it unto Haman the son of Hammedatha the Agagite, the Jew's enemy." (v.10)

The king delegated full power and authority to Haman in this situation. The king paid ten thousand talents of silver from the treasury to the individual Haman put in charge of the genocide. The publication was sent to all the king's military's top officials, governors, lieutenants, and rulers of all 127 provinces in every language, in the name of King Ahasuerus, and sealed with the king's ring.

It was so ordered that on the thirteenth day of March, the destruction of all Jews, regardless of age, and young, old, weak children and newborns, were slated for slaughter. A copy of the mandate was circulated to all the provinces to be ready on that day and ready to give up their life belongings. Signed, sealed, and delivered, the deal was publicized to all the Jews. Afterward, the king and Haman sat down for drinks after the agreement was signed. Killing someone seemed like a good idea! It was just like every other day.

CHAPTER FOUR

JEWS LAMENTATIONS

"...when the wicked beareth rule, the people mourn."
Proverbs 29:2

Upon hearing of the impending peril pronounced upon the Jews, Mordecai was stricken with grief. He ripped his clothes, put on sackcloth and ashes, and went out into the middle of the city with a loud, bitter cry. Then he went before the king's gate and sat there in sackcloth and ashes as an outward display of his revolt against what was happening.

Here we see another example of Mordecai's strong character and leadership. He was fearless, yet he was compassionate. He was not concerned about how he would be portrayed, nor did he feel any less of a man to go out into the city and express his anguish. He did not care who heard or saw him. He approached the king's gate clothed in sackcloth and stopped at the king's gate for no one could enter in sackcloth. *Ecclesiastes 3:4 says, A time to weep, and a time to laugh; a time to mourn, and a time to dance."* The time to mourn was now, right in front of the king's gate if necessary. David said, *"I cried unto God with my voice, even unto God with my voice; and he gave ear unto me." Psalms 77:1.*

This year, and worldwide, we were shattered by the death of half a million people due to an unknown virus. This virus spread worldwide, impacting people from all walks of life, cultures, and religions. There were no detainees. It shook people's livelihoods, economies, relationships, education, and everything else in their lives. I saw the people in Brazil were crying out to God for help, just like Mordecai did in the middle of the street, and kneeling on the sidewalks praying to God, "Please help us, LORD." We will never forget many events that happened this past year, and we will never be the same.

As we see in the Book of Esther, God never abandons His people. You can see how His providence, protection, and patience are ever working in the shadows, and nothing gets by Him without His all-knowing, all-seeing eye. That is why His name is not mentioned. Just because His name was not mentioned does not mean that He was not in their midst. We may not always recognize God's workings in our lives, but it does not mean He is not here. People worldwide seek God in the same way Esther did, saying, fast with me (until we hear from God.) Bible says *II Chronicles 20:9, "If, when evil cometh upon us, as the sword, judgment, or pestilence, or famine, we stand before this house, and in thy presence, (for thy name is in this house,) and cry unto thee in our affliction, then thou will hear and help."* The battle between good and evil continues. But we already know who the winner is.

Leadership On Display

Lying in sackcloth and ashes was symbolic of humiliation, grief, and repentance (Matt 11:21). Many of the prophets, priests, and people in biblical times publicly displayed their suffering by using this method. (1 Kings 20:31-32; 2 Kings 19:1) Sackcloth was a garment made from black goat's hair; it was coarse and uncomfortable. The ashes represented desolation and ruin. Accepting an ash cross on one's forehead signified our death and repentance [1]. It also represents Christ's 40 days of temptation in the desert, which gave him 40 days to prepare for his passion, death, and resurrection. Book of Genesis: *"You are dust, and to dust, you will return."*

Sitting at the king's gate in sackcloth was considered a bad omen, and it put the king on notice of what was going on made him aware that he could do something about it. However, some believe that it was not permitted because the king did not wish to hear about the people's troubles, see them, or learn about the origins of or protests occurring among the people. Mordecai wanted to make sure that the king was aware of his pain and what he felt over the mandate. Mordecai again exhibited fearlessness; he was unafraid of the consequences and was ready to protest. Mordecai was taking a stand against the unjust decree of genocide to take place on his people. Before Mordecai became a leader, he was a leader. He stood for the people and caused Esther to stand for the people as well.

When Esther heard that Mordecai was sitting at the king's

---

1 https://www.baltimoresun.com

gate in sackcloth, she sent Hatach (personal assistant appointed to her by the king) with clothes for Mordecai to put on, but Mordecai refused. He refused to be comforted and sent word back to Esther, outlining everything that happened, and the decree sent out against the Jews, including the hit money to be paid out of the treasury. Mordecai gave Hatach a copy of the order to show to Esther to see the seriousness and urgency of the matter. He commanded Esther to go to the king and beg for mercy to reverse this parody of injustice against the Jews.

When Esther received the decree Mordecai handed to her, Esther was grieved and pricked in her heart. Esther seemed to have been shielded from the outside world, as she seemed unaware of the decree. However, she informed Mordecai that the king had not called for her presence for thirty days. Anyone who goes before the king without an invitation could be put to death immediately. Mordecai did not want to hear any excuses or explanations.

"Then Mordecai commanded to answer Esther, Think not with thyself that thou shalt escape in the king's house, more than all the Jews. For if thou altogether holdest thy peace at this time, then shall their enlargement and deliverance arise to the Jews from another place;" (4:13-14)

This matter was of utmost urgency, and nothing was more important than the Jews' deliverance. He reminded Esther that this fight involved her as much as it did the Jews. She would not be able to escape. If deliverance did not come from Esther's hands,

Mordecai believed that God would find another way for the people to be delivered, but Esther and her Father's house would be ruined. *Psalms 94. "Fear not, for I am with you; Be not dismayed, for I am your God." Isaiah 41:10.* Esther immediately understood what she needed to do.

> *"But thou and thy father's house shall be destroyed: and who knoweth whether thou art come to the kingdom for such a time as this?"*

God raises people at certain times for specific reasons. You may not always have the luxury of rethinking your calling. When God opens doors and has spoken to you that it is your time, you need to step in before that door of opportunity closes. Esther sought the Lord to clarify what to do, even though her foster parent, whom she loved dearly, told her what she needed to do. She did not make a move until she heard from God.

This is an important reminder for our elected officials, particularly those from diverse backgrounds and people of color, who recognize that they would not be in their current positions if not for God. Is it possible that God has put you in that role to help "make things right"? God is the one who takes one down and replaces them with another.

THE ESTHER FAST THAT BROUGHT DELIVERANCE

"Consider ye, and call for the mourning women, that they may come; and send for skillful women that they may come." Jeremiah 9:17. Esther sent a message back to Mordecai saying,

organize the people together in Shushan to fast with me and my maidens for three days and three nights. Afterward, I will go before the king and advocate for the deliverance of our people. If I die in the process, so be it. (4:16) *"For whosoever will save his life shall lose it, but whosoever shall lose his life for my sake and the gospel's, the same shall save it." Mark 8:35. Some* things we fight for are not easy and are downright hard. Esther was in jeopardy of losing her life if she exposed the secret she had been keeping from the king all these years. Nonetheless, she was willing to reveal her secret to save her people. Esther fasted in preparation to answer God's call for her life. *Matthew 6:33 says, "But seek ye first the kingdom of God and his righteousness, and all these things shall be added unto you."* Esther was ready. She found strength in the battle. *"And I set my face unto the Lord God, to seek by prayer and supplications, with fasting, and sackcloth, and ashes..." Daniel 9:3 –*

The Bible tells us, "we must put on the whole armor of God to stand against the wiles of the devil." *"For we wrestle not against flesh and blood, but against principalities, against powers, against the rulers of the darkness of this world, against spiritual wickedness in high places." Ephesians 6:10-12.* Corporate Prayer and fasting are powerful. Before Esther sought the king's help, she went before the King of Kings first.

God will help you when you seek him first. God will stand with you in the fight. He will give you the strength and wisdom needed to do His will. Mordecai went his way and did all that

Toni Wright, Author

Esther commanded him to do.

CHAPTER FIVE

ESTHER'S FIRST BANQUET

"The king's heart is in the hand of the LORD, as the rivers of water: he turns it wherever he pleases." Proverbs 21:1

On the third day of Esther's fast, she was ready to take on the challenge for which God had called her. Dressed in royal attire, Esther stood in the inner court of the king's house, in plain sight of the king so he could see her. *"But ye are a chosen generation, a royal priesthood, a holy nation, a peculiar people; that ye should show forth the praises of him who hath called you out of darkness into his marvelous light." 1 Peter 2:9.* When the king looked up and saw Esther dressed in her royal apparel and standing in the inner court, he immediately granted her favor by holding out the golden scepter. Esther touched the king's scepter and received his favor. Esther did not reveal her true desires at the first banquet. The Bible did not tell us her motives for having the two meetings, but it may have likely been to understand the king's relationship with Haman.

When Esther touched the top of the king's scepter, she accepted the king's favor toward her. God has stretched out His hands open wide to us, and all we must do is receive His favor, His grace, and His invitation to be whole. When we reach out to God, we touch the heart of the King of Kings, and we have received God's favor in our lives. He never gets weary of us coming to Him for help. The king asked Esther to repeat her plea, promising to give her half of the kingdom if she did. For now, Esther only revealed that she wanted a second banquet.

QUEEN ESTHER'S SPECIAL BANQUET REQUEST

Esther was not shy about telling the king what she wanted. She requested the king's and Haman's presence at a second banquet she prepared for them. The king said, "Tell Haman to hurry and come to the banquet that Esther has prepared." So, the king and Haman joined Esther at the first banquet which she had prepared. The king said to Esther, "what is thy petition? Whatever you want, I will give it to you even to the half of the kingdom." Jesus says, *"If ye shall ask anything in my name, I will do it." St. John 14:14.* Esther requested a second banquet with the king and Haman's presence.

"If I have found favor in the sight of the king, and if it please the king to grant my petition, and to perform my request, let the king and Haman come to the banquet that I shall prepare for them, and I will do tomorrow as the king hath said." (5:14)

Esther's communication style and approach to the king won her his favor and love. This is not just a touchy feeling evaluation. He offered her half of the kingdom on more than one occasion, and he never asked her to parade around in the nude.

1 Peter 3:1-2 reminds us that "when we use wisdom and humility with our husbands, even if they are not Christians, they will be won over by our chaste and respectful behavior. They will not be won by our outward beauty only...." **(Paraphrased)** Believe me, and sometimes this is a hard pill to swallow for some of us. Esther requested the presence of the king and Haman at a second banquet. The Bible does not say why she requested the banquets in two parts. Haman was overwhelmed with joy for being invited to a banquet with the king and queen. He ran home to tell his wife and friends but was stopped short in his tracks when he saw Mordecai. Mordecai did not look up, neither did he stand up, nor did he move as Haman was passing by. He knew how to get under Haman's skin, and Haman got under his skin.

Haman paused but then rushed home to tell his wife and friends of the good news that he was invited to a second banquet with the queen. As Haman was bragging to his wife about all the blessings the King bestowed upon him, he stopped short of complaining that it did not mean anything if Mordecai was still alive and sitting at the king's gate. This is what hate does to people? We see it every day when we turn on our televisions? Hate is like cancer; it eats away at you from the inside out and destroys your soul. People with hate in their hearts are miserable.

Haman's wife, Zeresh (whose name means "misery), Haman's wife was just as wicked as Haman and suggested to Haman to build 50-foot-high gallows and hang Mordecai on the gallows before the banquet starts. She further instructed Haman to arrive to work early the next day to meet with the king before attending the feast of wine so that Haman could sit down and eat his meal in peace. Haman agreed and the next day arrived at the banquet early so he could speak with the king about hanging Mordecai.

CHAPTER SIX

THE KING'S PLAN TO HONOR MORDECAI

"No weapon that is formed against thee shall prosper, and every tongue that shall rise against thee in judgment thy shall condemn. This is the heritage of the servants of the LORD, and their righteousness is of me, saith the LORD." Isaiah 54:17.

While the enemy is plotting your downfall, God is plotting your promotion. When God has a plan for your life, the enemy cannot stop it. What God has for you is for you, and no one can take it away from you. *Revelations 3:8-9 I know thy works: behold, I have set before thee an open door, and no man can shut it: for thou hast a little strength, and hast kept my word and hast not denied my name. Behold, I will make them of the synagogue of Satan, which say they are Jews, and are not, but do lie; behold, I will make them to come and worship before thy feet, and to know that I have loved thee." (Mordecai)*

NEVER UNDERESTIMATE GOD'S TIMING

The enemy's attacks often overshadow God's love and compassion for His people. As your foes plan your demise, God is preparing a path for you in the wilderness. *Psalms 71: -11, "For my enemies speak against me, and those who lie in wait for my life conspire, saying, "God has forsaken him; pursue him and seize him, for there is no one to rescue him."* WRONG! Haman was on his way to do Mordecai harm, but little did he know that God looks out for His own. *Isaiah 54:17 says, "No weapon that is formed against thee shall prosper, and every tongue that shall rise against thee in judgment thou shalt condemn. This is the heritage of the servants of the LORD, and their righteousness is of me, saith the LORD."*

The night before the banquet, the king had insomnia and asked that the Book of records be read to him. It was their custom that when someone did something deserving, the king rewarded faithful service to the person. This could be very embarrassing for the king if the person were not adequately rewarded, especially if that person saved the king's life.

Never underestimate God's providence, and timing is omnipresence; God never forgets. (According to commentary, this was about five years later.) But while Haman was building the gallows for Mordecai, the king made a strategy to honor Mordecai. Keeping a book of the chronicles or records was a method all kings did. God also keeps a Book of Remembrance, and when we speak the truth about God or praise Him to one another, that Book is opened, and God remembers us. *"Then they that feared the Lord spake often one to another: and the Lord hearkened, and heard it, and a book of remembrance was written before him for them that feared the Lord, and that thought upon his name. And they shall be mine, saith the Lord of hosts, in that day when I make up my jewels; and I will spare them, as a man spareth his own son that serveth him." Malachi 3:16*

MORDECAI DID NOT SEEK PRAISE

Hebrews 6:10 reminds us, "For God is not unrighteous to forget your work and labor of love, which ye have shewed toward his name..." "Has Mordecai received some recognition for this deed?" the king inquired. "No," replied the king's servants. The king asked who was in the outer courts before the banquet began. Haman was rumored to be in the courtroom. Remember how Haman's wife advised him to arrive early to build a gallows for Mordecai? "All right, let him in," the king said. He posed a hypothetical question to Haman about how to honor someone who impressed the king. Who else could he be thinking of other than himself? Haman reasoned, who is better than me? For this, Haman devised a complex and lavish blessing. However, I got the impression from reading his list that Haman aspired to be king. He may have been behaving with good conscience.

A Man Ought Not To Think More Highly Of Himself Than He Should

"What should be done for the man whom the king adores?" Haman answered when the king asked what should be done for the man whom the king adores. Haman could not imagine the king was not talking about anyone else. After all, there was no one greater in Haman's eyes than himself. Before he was questioned, it seems that he had already contemplated or rehearsed this answer. He immediately understood what to suggest."

Haman's Kingly List:

- Let the royal apparel be brought, *which the king used* to wear.
- And the horse that the *king rides on every day.*
- And the *crown the king puts on his head every day.*
- Let this apparel and the horse be delivered to the hand of one the king's most noble princes, that they **may dress the man** withal whom the king delights to honor and bring him on horseback through the street of the city and proclaim before him, "Thus shall it be done to the man whom the king delights to honor."

To Be Like The King

We should all strive to be like the King. "To Be Like Jesus, What I

Want Is to Be Like Him," as the song goes. That is what it feels like Haman is doing, at least. Everything on his list was modeled after the king's possessions. It would be frightening if Haman desired these things because he genuinely desired to be the "king." I am not sure if Haman's intentions were genuinely innocent, but it was a privilege to aspire to be like the king.

The Bible tells us, *"Let another man praise thee, and not thine own mouth; a stranger, and not thine own lips." Proverbs 27:2.*

HAMAN FORCED TO GET A REALITY CHECK

Psalms 37:12-13 "The wicked plotteth against the just, and gnasheth upon him with his teething. The Lord shall laugh at him: for he seeth that his day is coming." After Haman finished his elaborate list of "kingly" desires, the king said, bring Haman to me now. The king had other designs for Mordecai before Haman could approach him with his plot to hang him on the gallows he had designed. The king commanded Haman to do as he has said unto Mordecai. Hurry, complete everything you have said, and leave no stone unturned. *"Pride goeth before destruction, and a haughty spirit before a fall." Proverbs 16:18.*

Through the streets they went, Haman proclaiming Mordecai as the one the king favored. Mordecai, humble as ever, never said a word. After it was over, Mordecai went back to his post guarding the king's gate while Haman picked up his deflated ego and ran home to tell his wife and friends all that happened.

David said in *Psalms 37:35, "I have seen the wicked in great power and spreading himself like a green bay tree. Yet he passed away, and, lo, he was not: yea, I sought him, but he could not be found."* It is good to know that God looks out for his people. He did not say you would not go through difficulty or how long you would go through, but He did promise that He would have pity and bring you out. *James 5:11 "Behold, we count them happy which endure. Ye have heard of the patience of Job, and have seen the end of the Lord; that the Lord is very pitiful, and of tender mercy."*

"Cast not away, therefore your confidence, which hath great recompense of reward."

I love the way *Acts 5:39* puts it, *"But if it is from God, you will not be able to overthrow them. You may even find yourselves fighting against God!"*

For indeed, as the saying goes, **"He may not come when you want Him to, but He will be right on time."** God's timing could not have been better. Sometimes we try to take the spirituality out of the text, but no one can set the tone for a blessing better than our heavenly Father. There are no coincidences. There are only blessings, mercy, and God's favor.

EVERYBODY MUST FACE THE KING ALONE

Haman told Zeresh, his wife, and all his friends what happened to him. Then Haman's "wise men" and his wife said, If Mordecai is of the seed of the Jews, before whom thou hast begun to fall, thou shalt not prevail against him, but shalt surely fall before him." (13) And while they were yet talking with him, the king's chamberlains were at the door to bring Haman unto the banquet that Esther had prepared. Isn't it ironic that the same people who instructed Haman to hang Mordecai are the same people who are now predicting that if he went up against the Jews, he would lose?

Conversational Thought

This is a valuable lesson to learn, particularly for young people. Your "buddies" will urge you to do something wrong, but when you get caught, you are on your own, and they will say, "You should have known better." Or, if the enemy persuades you to do something wrong, he won't be there when things go wrong. You will have to meet the judge on your own. Those who persuaded Haman to build a gallows to hang Mordecai suddenly realized that if Mordecai were a Jew, Haman would fail.

CHAPTER SEVEN

QUEEN ESTHER REVEALS HER ADVERSARY

"The LORD knoweth the thoughts of man, that they are vanity. For the LORD will not cast off his people, neither will he forsake his inheritance. And he shall bring upon them their own iniquity and shall cut them off in their own wickedness."

BANQUET TWO-JUDGEMENT DAY

Haman realized that his reign of terror was coming to an end. He immediately went with the king's men to the second banquet with the queen and king. During the Banquet of Wine, while relaxing and having their drinks, the king asked Esther again to reveal her desire. This time Esther does not hold. She says,

"If I have found favor in thy sight, O king, and if it please the king, let my life be given me at my petition, and my people at my request: for we are sold, I and my people, to be destroyed, to be slain, and to perish. But if we had been sold for bondmen and bondwomen, I had held my tongue, although the enemy could not offset the king's damage."

It is no wonder the king was so smitten with Esther. She knew how to finesse her words. She knew exactly how to address the king, and she knew what to say and how to say it. Sometimes when we go before God, we do not always know what to say. *Hosea 14:2 tells us, "Take with you words and return to the Lord..."* Esther employed soft-spoken, influencing, and honorable words with the king. As the scripture says, she took with her words, and the king's heart was turned to her. The king, like any protective, loving husband, was beside himself. He says to the Queen, *"Who is this, and where is he that dare think he is bold enough to get away with this?"*

HAMAN'S EVIL LEGACY ENDS

Esther probably jumps up and points to Haman and says, *"The adversary is this wicked Haman."* Haman knew he was in trouble at this point, and fear gripped his heart in a way he had never experienced before. When the king heard that it was Haman, he was infuriated. He had to go out to the palace garden to gain some composure. After all, this was the king's vizier, his top official. His confidante, someone the king trusted, had his back. A man he had just given a powerful promotion to that ranked only second to himself. To hear this devastating news was enough, but when he came back in, he saw Haman was crouched before the queen, and he perceived that Haman was attacking the queen (in front of everybody). He said, "will you also force yourself on her in my house?" Immediately, his men covered Haman's face. (Covering the perpetrator's face was a Persian custom that meant the king did not want to see that person's face anymore. It meant "kill him.")[2] (also see 2 Kings 4:27) One of the king's chamberlain said, "Haman just built a 50-foot-high gallows made specifically for Mordecai, the same man who saved your life, is standing in the house of Haman. Then the king said, "Hang him on it." Haman was hanged, and he was no more. Then was the king's wrath appeased.

Unfortunately, sometimes the evil set-in motion is not over when that person dies or leaves a position. There is still work that needs to occur to reverse, alter, or eliminate what the perpetrator instigated. David said, *"...yet he passed away and was no more; though I looked for him he could not be found." Psalms 37:36.*

"If you dig one ditch, you better dig two cause the trap you set just may be for you." Mahalia Jackson an[3]

Some people don't care about the legacy they leave behind. They are proud to be evil, but evil comes at a price. They may be smiling now, but only because God's time has not arrived yet. The Bible says, *"Everyone who is arrogant (proud) in heart is an abomination (disgrace) to the LORD: be assured, he shall not be*

---

[2] "Caput obnubito" Ciceron. Orat. 18. "pro Rabirio", Kuv, Hist. I. 1. P.15. Curt. Hist. I. 6. C. 11. Vid. Solerium de Pileo, sect. 2. P. 20.

[3] Mahalia Jackson, an American singer and songwriter

unpunished." Psalms 16:5 ESV)

"Though hand join in hand, the wicked shall not be unpunished: but the seed of the righteous shall be delivered." Proverbs 11:21. It does not matter how strong, how mighty, how slick the proud think they are; God knows their calamity is coming."

1 John 4:20 - "If a man says, I love God, and hateth his brother, he is a liar; for he, that loveth not his brother whom he has seen, how can he love God whom he hath not seen?"

It does not matter your ethnicity, your educational background, the color of skin, your demographics, or your social and economic background, and God has commanded us to love. Haman spent most of his time hating the Jews and plotting their demise. Haman's pride would be his downfall. His only concern was for himself, how he could become significant in his own eyes and the eyes of his followers. When the Jews people did not accommodate his ego, he vowed to destroy them. He felt like they did not even deserve to breathe the same air he breathed. By the way, the air that God provides. It was pride, and pride goes before a fall. All living creatures are created by and belong to God. He created life for his purpose and His plan. *"For all that is in the world, the lust of the flesh, and the lust of the eyes, and the pride of life, is not of the Father, but is of the world."*

This kind of arrogance can be found all the time in the boardrooms and backrooms of proud and evil people. People who despise others because of their culture, faith, or some other excuse feel they have legitimate cause for their hate. They make decisions on how they can destroy another person, taking on the position of God. They sit down after boasting about killing and lift a toast to one another to celebrate murder. But God said, "my glory will I share with no man." All souls belong to God.

But the Bible says, *"I am the LORD: that is my name: and my glory will I not give to another, neither my praise to graven images."*

"I will laugh at their calamity; I will mock when their fear comes." Proverbs 1:26-28

"Humble yourselves, therefore, under the mighty hand of God so that at the proper time he may exalt you..." 1 Peter 5:6-7.

GOD IS THE CREATOR OF ALL LIFE

"For God so loved the world that He gave His only begotten Son, that whosoever believeth in him should not perish, but have everlasting life." John 3:16.

Ezekiel 18:4 "Behold, all souls are mine: as the soul of the father, so also the soul of the son is mine: the soul that sinneth, it shall die."

"And fear not them which kill the body but are not able to kill the soul: but rather fear him which is able to destroy both soul and body in hell." Matthew 10:28.

CHAPTER EIGHT

MORDECAI IS GIVEN HAMAN'S WEALTH

Promotion Comes from God

"A good man leaveth an inheritance to his children's children: and the wealth of the sinner is laid up for the just." Proverbs 13:22

Not only did the king honor Esther's request by hanging Haman on the gallows Haman had built for Mordecai, He gave the house of Haman to Esther. *"He who digs a pit will fall into it, and he who rolls a stone will have it rolled back on him." Proverbs 26:27.* After Esther told the king who Mordecai was to her and how he had raised her as his daughter, the king had much respect for Mordecai and took off the signet ring he had once given to Haman Chapter three and gave it to Mordecai. Esther then put Mordecai in charge of all that Haman owned, including his home, job, money, authority, and everything. I must pause right here and say, "what a mighty God we serve." *"You intended to harm me, but God intended it all for good. Joseph said, He brought me to this position so I could save the lives of many people." Genesis 50:20 (NIV)* I know some things we do not understand while they are happening, but God has a way of making it up to us and making every crooked way straight before our face. Some of the things we have experienced in our lifetime are shocking, though it is no surprise to our God. "Cast not away, therefore, your confidence. God will reward us in His time, and in His way."

MADE A WAY OUT OF NO WAY

Esther made one more appeal before the king, imploring the king with tears in her eyes that he would revoke the heinous plot the vile Haman had conceived against the Jews. However, the king explained once a decree is sealed with his royal ring, it could not be reversed. However, a new order could be written declaring whatever you want. *"If it please the king, and if I have found favor in your sight, and the thing seem right to you, and if I am pleasing in your eyes, let it be written to reverse the letters devised by Haman ... which he wrote to destroy the Jews which are in all the king's provinces."* **(Paraphrased)** *"For how can I endure seeing the evil that shall come unto my people? Or how can I endure to see the destruction of my kindred?"*

Sometimes when we want something bad enough, we must come before God in bold humility, and we will find help in a time of need. Esther could have said, "well, he said no last time, so I will not ask again. But she came before the king again until she received an answer. The Bible tells us to, *"I have set watchmen upon thy walls, O Jerusalem, which shall never hold their peace day nor night: ye that make mention of the LORD keep not silence (give yourselves no rest). And give him no rest, till he establish, and till he makes Jerusalem a praise in the earth". Isaiah 62:6-7*

The Bible also tells us, *"The Lord is near to those who are discouraged; he saves those who have lost all hope." (GNT) "...unto them that are of a broken heart; and saveth such as be of a contrite spirit." (KJV)*

Esther's posture of falling at the king's feet symbolizes falling at Jesus' feet in humble reverence and submission. *The king could not resist Esther's humble attitude and gave her the power and authority to rewrite what the devil has plotted against them.*

I Have Given You What You Need to Win

The king reminded Esther and Mordecai of the power he had put in their hands. Mordecai and Esther learned they had to use the power of the ring. They were still relying on the king, but the king had to remind them that he had given them the power (the ring) and the authority to use his name (again to rewrite their destiny). (Esther was close to the king, always in communication with him and falling at his feet with tears.) "So, King Xerxes said to Esther the Queen and Mordecai the Jew, *"Behold, I have given Haman's estate to Esther, and he was hanged on the gallows because he attacked the Jews. Now you may write in the king's name as you please regarding the Jews, and seal it with the royal signet ring. For a decree that is written in the name of the king and sealed with the royal signet ring cannot be revoked." (BSB)* When they caught this revelation, they were changed for life. They got busy and had the scribes write what they needed the people to do.

NO ONE CAN REVERSE WHAT YOU SAY

The Bible says the power of life and death is in your tongue. *"Death and life are in the power of the tongue, And those who love it will eat its fruit." Proverbs 18:21 (NKJV)* Jesus has given us the authority to use His name. *"For verily I say unto you, That whosoever shall say unto this mountain, Be thou removed, and be thou cast into the sea; and shall not doubt in his heart but shall believe that those things which he saith shall come to pass; he shall have whatsoever he saith." Mark 11:23.* The Holy Spirit has been entrusted to us so that we may speak in His name. Perhaps we are simply too lazy to speak it out or too silent to speak in the Lord's name at times. You may believe it, but you remain silent. (Just a Thought)

Then Jesus said, *"If ye shall ask anything in my name, I will do it." John 14:14.* When we use his name, and something does not happen when we think it should occur, we get discouraged and think it did not work. That is when Satan steps in and says to you, "see, it did not work." But Satan is a liar, and he cannot stop what God has ordained. Numbers 23:20, "Behold, I have received commandment to bless: and he hath blessed; I cannot reverse it." The king told Esther, *"whatever you write, it cannot be reversed because it is in my name."* Jesus said the same thing.

Are you proclaiming what shall come to pass? Do you believe God for those things that you believe you shall have? Are you speaking it, writing it, confessing it? Get the Journal to this book and write in Jesus' name what you want Him to do for you.

THE RIGHT TO FIGHT

Immediately, the king's scribes were summoned to rewrite all that Mordecai commanded of the Jews and to the lieutenants, deputies, and rulers of the provinces from India to Ethiopia. According to their language, everyone received a letter in writing sealed with the king's name and royal ring. They got busy, and the letters were sent by horseback, mules, camels, and young dromedaries. The king granted the Jews in every city to assemble, stand for their life, destroy, kill, and conquer all the power and province that would assault them. They were given the authority to protect their little ones and women and take anything they wanted of the spoil as a possession.

Signed, sealed, and delivered, they were granted the right to fight for their families. It reminds me of when your mama used to tell you, "don't come back in this house. You better not let anybody beat up your sister or your brother. Go back out there and fight!" (oops!) They did not allow you to run from your enemy. They also did not let you start fights either!

Unify, Unify, Unify

The Jews began to unify themselves and were ready against that day to avenge themselves of their enemies. In the Book of Nehemiah, Nehemiah told the people, *"...Do not be afraid of them. Remember the LORD, who is great and awesome, and fight for your brothers, your sons, your daughters, your wives, and your homes." Nehemiah 4:14.*

Take A Stand for What is Right

Ephesians 6:12 "Finally, my brethren, be strong in the Lord, and in the power of his might. Put on the whole armor of God, that ye may be able to stand against the wiles of the devil. For we wrestle not against flesh and blood, but against principalities, against powers, against the rulers of the darkness of this world, against spiritual wickedness in high places. Wherefore take unto you the whole armor of God, that ye may be able to withstand in the evil day, and having done all, to stand. Stand therefore, having your loins girt about with truth, and having on the breastplate of righteousness..."

We must remind ourselves from time to time that we are engaged in spiritual warfare. It was easy to go out there and fight with our fists, sticks, and (well, you get the idea.) But spiritual warfare is an acquired "taste." At least it was for me. It takes experience (lots of fights) to learn how to win, learn how to do battle, and still learn. But fighting an enemy that you cannot always see coming is a different kind of battle. That is why David said, *"If it had not been the LORD who was on our side, ... when the enemy rose up against us: Then they had swallowed us up quick when their wrath was kindled against us:" Psalms 124:1-3.*

Esther understood from the beginning that this was a fight that she must involve the Lord of Hosts. She immediately went to God because she knew this was not going to be an ordinary fight. She knew she could not do this in her strength. Everyone that would be in the battle needed to align themselves with the war by fasting. She wanted to win; they had to win. She said, "tell the people to fast with me and my maidens." It is incredible to see the young people picking up the battle cry, speaking out, protesting, and doing what they can do. Esther won her battle by FIRST going to God and finding the strength, wisdom, and favor to win. This is a lesson for me and all of us. He is a very present help in times of trouble. He is the only one who can aid us in our fight against wickedness in high places and against these demonic spirits and principalities. *St. John 15:5 "I am the vine, ye are the branches: he that abideth in me, and I in Him, the same bringeth forth much fruit: for without me ye can do nothing."* We are connected to the vine, Jesus, and His word lives in us. We cannot do anything without Him.

Mordecai Out of the Shadows

Esther put Mordecai in his rightful place of authority. She returned the favor to Mordecai, who had taken her in and raised her to be the heroine she was. She stood by him and helped him come from the shadows to the forefront as the Jewish people's captain. The people loved and respected Mordecai and honored him for his leadership. The Bible says, *"When the righteous are in authority, the people rejoice: but when the wicked beareth rule, the people mourn." Proverbs 29:2.* When the wicked rule, there is nothing but confusion, chaos, and anarchy. God is not the author of confusion.

Mordecai went out of the king's presence dressed in his royal apparel of blue and white, and with a great crown of gold, and with a garment of fine linen and purple: and the city of Shushan rejoiced and was glad. The Bible says that there was hope, gladness, joy, and honor. There was no chaos; he was honest and ruled the people with hope and goodness. He did not rule with an iron fist, he was not trying to garner wealth and attention for himself, and the Jews were pleased.

CHAPTER NINE

HE ALWAYS CAUSES ME TO TRIUMPH

"Now thanks be unto God, which always causeth us to triumph in Christ, and maketh manifest the savour of his knowledge by us in every place." 2 Corinthians 2:14

THE JEWS CELEBRATE

"Blessed be the LORD my strength, which teaches my hands to war, and my fingers to fight: My goodness, and my fortress; my high tower, and my deliverer; my shield, and He in whom I trust; who subdueth my people under me." Psalms 144:1.

On the thirteenth day of the twelfth month, the time had come for the decree's declaration's execution. Deuteronomy 20:1-4 tells us, "When thou goest out to battle against thine enemies, and seest horses, and chariots, and a people more than thou, be not afraid of them: for the Lord thy God is with thee...And it shall be, when ye are *come nigh unto the battle...against your enemies let not your hearts faint, fear not, and do not tremble, neither be ye terrified because of them; For the Lord your God is he that goeth with you, to fight for you against your enemies, to save you."*

The LORD of Host was with them in their fight against their adversaries. They also had the power of King Ahasuerus behind them and the forces of the armies of the provinces, the lieutenants, deputies, and the king's officers. *"And when the servant of the man of God was risen early, and gone forth, behold, a host compassed the city both with horses and chariots. And his servant said unto him, Alas, my master! How shall we do? And he answered, Fear not: for they that be with us are more than they that be with them." II Kings 6:16.*

VICTORIES, VICTORIES AND MORE VICTORIES

"Through God, we shall do valiantly: for he shall tread down our enemies." Psalms 108:13. The Jews overtook their adversary and won a crushing victory over them. They slew all their foes with a single sword stroke and defended themselves from all who hated them. Those who attempted to kill them were defeated. Many were converted and became Jews as Mordecai's reputation spread across the provinces and the king's palace.

Day One: In Susa, the citadel, the Jews killed five hundred men and the ten sons of Haman, but they did not touch the enemy's spoil.

Day Two: The king reported to Esther and enquired how the

battle went in other areas of the province? Whatever Esther requested, the king was obliged to give it to her because he loved her. Esther asked that Haman's ten sons hang on the same gallows as their father. The king so ordered that Haman's ten sons hang on the gallows alongside their father.

CONVERSATIONAL THOUGHT

Throughout this battle, the king and Esther communicated consistently, more than they have ever spoken before. The secret was out that she was a Jew, and these were her people. But that did not stop the king from loving her, and it seems maybe he loved her even more. When we are in the midst of the storm, we must communicate with God as much as possible and reveal any secrets we may have. He already understands, so we must open ourselves up to Him so that He can complete the task at hand.

The king was concerned with how things were going, so he checked in with Esther every day, asking her what else she needed to win the battle. (v 12) He was not asking her if she needed another royal outfit, or another crown, or something material. **He wanted to know what do you need to win this battle?** What else does God need to help you win your current battle? What else can God do to assist you? What is God's question? What do you need to remain whole? Do you need a deeper understanding of God's Word? Do you need additional strength? Do you want more of my Spirit, joy, or the correct viewpoint?

Lord, Don't Move the Mountain

I think the song goes something like this, "Lord Don't Move the Mountain But Give Me the Strength To Climb It." I am just like a lot of you; that is not always my prayer. But when the king asked Esther to make a request, this time Esther did not ask, "to remove, the edict against them, but she asked for the heads of the sons of Haman. Leave no prisoners. She asked for victory in the fight." She was focused, aggressive and uncompromising with the enemy. She was not going to give them a chance to recoup and come back to finish destroying them.

The Battle Is Already Won

On the fourteenth day of the month of Adar, three hundred men were slang in Shushan, but they refused to lay hold of the enemy's prey. Haman's ten sons hanged, and as before, they laid not their hands on any of the spoils. Other Jews in the king's provinces unified and fought to protect their families by fighting in yet the bloodiest battle of all, killing 75,000 of their enemies, leaving behind the spoils.

Why is that so important not to take the enemy's spoil? It is my understanding, and I may not have the full story here, but we read in *1 Samuel the 15th Chapter, the LORD of hosts, said "I remember that which Amalek did to Israel, how he waited for him in the cut (slang) when he came up from Egypt. Now go and smite Amalek, and destroy all that they have, and spare them not but Saul and the people disobeyed and spared Agag, and the best sheep, oxen, fatlings, lambs, and all that was good, and would not utterly destroy them."* Mordecai did not tell them not to take the enemies to spoil, but maybe they did not take the spoil because of the Lord's command to Saul and Saul's disobedience.

DURING THE MIDST OF BATTLE

When you are fighting a battle, you are never alone, and you are never alone. While it might seem that God is absent, God vowed that he would never leave you. *1 John 4:4 says, "greater is he that is within me than he that is in the world."* God is greater than any circumstances or any enemies you face. *Romans 8:31* reminds us that, *"...If God be for us, who can be against us?"* You cannot allow fear to paralyze you from fighting the good fight of faith. The enemy is always trying to magnify himself to be greater than he is to keep you intimidated, hopeless, and afraid. The Jews' adversaries had between nine and eleven months to terrorize and put fear in the Jews.

SET YOUR MIND FOR BATTLE

"For the Lord, your God is he that goeth with you, to fight for you against your enemies, to save you." Deuteronomy 20:4
The devil wants you to believe you will not prevail, but when have you known the devil to speak the truth? In the end, God always gives us victory. *II Kings 6:6-17 Elisha answered, 'Fear not: for they that be with us are more than they that be with them. And Elisha prayed, and said, Lord, I pray thee, open his eyes, that he*

may see. And the Lord opened the eyes of the young man; and he saw: and behold, the mountain was full of horses and chariots of fire round about Elisha."

Often, we need our spiritual eyes to be opened so that we can see "the salvation of the Lord with us." When everything is said and done, we will emerge more than a conqueror, no matter what it looks like or how loud and boisterous the enemy becomes. *Romans 8:37 say, "Nay, in all these things we are more than conquerors through him that loved us."* And nothing shall separate us from the love of God. (Rom 8:38-39) When we trust God, He will cause our enemies to flee before us seven ways. He said, *"A thousand shall fall at thy side, and ten thousand at thy right hand; but it shall not come nigh thee. Psalms 91:7 "Now thanks be unto God, which always causes us to triumph in Christ, and maketh manifest (through us) the savor (fragrance) of his knowledge by us in every place." 2 Corinthians 2:14*

The Feast of Purim

Purim (Hebrew word for "Lots") is a tradition celebrated by the Jewish people commemorating the survival of the Jews who, in the 5th century B.C.E., were marked for distinction by the evil ruler Haman (although he was not alone in his quest.) The Jews came together on the thirteenth day, and on the fourteenth, they rested. On the fifteenth day of the month of Adar (March), they celebrated, making it a day of relaxing, eating, and celebrating. Mordecai's terror gripped them all, and many Jews converted to Jewish.

Mordecai was the man of the hour, the man known for not bowing to the enemy, Haman. He had a good reputation, and the people loved him. *The Bible says, "When the wicked rise, people hide themselves, but when they perish, the righteous increase. Proverbs 28:28*

CELEBRATE YOUR VICTORIES

The Jews of the villages that dwelt in the unwalled towns made the fourteenth day a day of gladness and feasting and a good day of sending portions to one another. Mordecai sent out letters documenting the victories that happened in all the king's provinces, both near and far, to establish among the Jews that they should keep the fourteenth day and the fifteenth day, yearly, as the days the Jews rested from all their enemies. The month that turned their sorrow into joy and their mourning into gladness: These would be days of celebrating through feasting and joy, and sending portions one to another, and giving gifts to the poor.

LADY ESTHER, MORE THAN A PRETTY FACE

Esther proved to be more than just a pretty face. Esther put in place Mordecai to lead the people to battle, and they conquered their enemies.

God's divine intervention thwarted Haman's plan to kill the Jews. The Jews commemorated these historic days in all the provinces as the Lord delivered the Jews. The Lord turned their grief into joy and their mourning into a day of celebration. The fourteenth day became a mandated holiday to commemorate deliverance from their enemies. That is why they called this day Purim after the name of Pur. This day was to be celebrated every year, even in various Jewish cultures throughout the world.

Esther and Mordecai, the Dynamic Duo, authorized and confirmed the writing of the letters of Purim. The letters were sent to everyone in the one hundred and twenty-seven provinces of King Ahasuerus, with words of peace and prosperity, to affirm the days of Purim.

Purim Is Celebrated

When Haman's name is mentioned in the Book of Esther, the people mock, sneer, stomp their feet, and make a loud noise to drown out Haman's name. *"Therefore, it shall be, when the LORD thy God hath given thee rest from all thine enemies round about, in the land which the LORD thy God giveth thee for an inheritance to possess it, that thou shalt blot out the remembrance of Amalek from under heaven; thou shalt not forget it." Deuteronomy 25:19.*

The Bible tells us in *Psalms 126:1*, *"When the Lord turned again the captivity of Zion; we were like them that dream. Then was our mouth filled with laughter, and our tongue with singing then said they among the heathen, The Lord hath done great things for them. The Lord hath done great things for us; whereof we are glad. Turn again our captivity, O Lord, as the streams in the south."*

STONES OF REMEMBRANCE

How many times do you praise God for bringing deliverance to our situation? Do something unique for yourself and brag about the Lord's goodness in your life. If God brought you through something and gave you a victory, big or small, celebrate. This is an excellent lesson to learn: Rejoice, thank God and do something that will remind you of the Lord's hand in your life. We tend to forget when the blessing is not astronomical. When you celebrate and are grateful for small victories, God will surely give more significant wins.

In Joshua 4:21, the Bible says, "And he spoke unto the children of Israel, saying, when your children shall ask their fathers in time to come, saying, What mean these stones? Then ye shall let your children know, saying Israel came over this Jordan on dry land. For the LORD your God dried up the waters of Jordan from before you, until ye passed over, as the LORD your God did to the Red sea, which he dried up from before us, until we were gone over: That all the people of the earth might know the hand of the LORD, that it is mighty: that ye might fear the LORD your God forever."

Memorializing God's deliverance in your life helps you to remember how good He has been in your life, and you can pass that on to your children and your children's children.

Another excellent lesson to learn here was the behavior of the Jews when they were delivered. They celebrated one another as a unified team and *gave gifts to one another and the poor.* They were happy for one another because they realized they were all in the fight together. No man is an island, and it is incredible to recognize not only your victory but the victory of someone else.

"Do not neglect to do good and to share what you have, for such sacrifices are pleasing to God." Hebrews 13:16.

"Whoever is generous to the poor lends to the LORD, and he will repay him for his deed." Proverbs 19:17.

The Jews rejoiced when they received their victory over their enemies.

"Rejoice in the Lord always: and again, I say, Rejoice." Philippians 4:4.

"Many are the afflictions of the righteous, but God delivers them out of them all."

"Evil shall slay the wicked: and they that hate the righteous shall be desolate." Psalms 34:19, 21.

Some people express their thanks by writing in a journal, like the one that accompanies this book. What a blessing it is to write down your successes and go back years later and read them. You will be surprised how much you forget. "Do not despise the day of small things."

CHAPTER TEN

THE DYNAMIC DUO

Psalms 75:6-7 "For promotion cometh neither from the east, nor from the west, nor from the south. But God is the judge: he putteth down one, and setteth up another."

Ahasuerus paid tribute to the land and the sea islands. All Mordecai's acts, power, and might, and the king's honor to Mordecai are recorded in the Book of the Kings of Media and Persia. Because of Mordecai's bravery in standing up against evil, and the many other good deeds he did, he was honored. In terms of influence and power, Mordecai was second only to the king. He quickly rose in popularity among the people and was well-liked.

The Feast Of Purim

Purim is a Jewish holiday commemorating the Jews deliverance Haman, an Achaemenid Persian Empire official who was planning to kill all the Jews, as recounted in the Book of Esther above.

1. Also called Festival of Lots
2. Jewish holiday commemorating the saving of the Jewish people from destruction instituted by their arch enemy Haman
3. Haman was the royal vizier to King Ahasuerus
4. Celebrated by days of feasting, gladness, and sending portions to one another, and giving to the poor
5. Reading and reciting the Book of Esther
6. Purim is celebrated annually on the 14th day of the Hebrew month of Adar (March)
7. In some cities, Purim was celebrated on the 15th of the month of Adar. The Feast of Purim is read and celebrated until this day.
8. When Haman's name is read out loud, they stomped their feet and shouted with loud voices, making loud noises to blot out the name of Haman.
9. According to Esther 9:31-32, the 13th day of Adar Purim was observed with the Esther fast

Seven Attributes to Look for In This Story

1. <u>God's Providence:</u> Esther went through a traumatic childhood, but God never took His watchful eyes off her. God sees our past, present, and future. He will never abandon nor forsake us. He loves us with everlasting love. Nothing is hidden from him. *(Proverbs 15:3. Ecclesiastes 12:13-14)*

2. <u>Courage:</u> Esther called a fast, at which time God gave her the courage to face her many adversaries. Courage can appear in many ways. Esther demonstrated courage by disclosing her identity to the King. She also showed bravery by appearing before the King without an invitation. Esther revealed courage in many other ways throughout the Book of Esther. *(Psalms 31:24; Ephesians 6:10-18)*

3. <u>God's Mercy</u>: God did not blame nor judge Israel for their failures or condemn them for being in their current situation. He is a forgiving and merciful God. Sometimes, people believe that God may withhold deliverance from them because they did something wrong. However, God is gracious and compassionate toward the just and the unjust. *(Psalms 136:1; Lamentations 3:22-23)*

4. <u>Jehovah-Jireh</u>: God provided the people of God with all they needed to triumph in their battle with their adversary. God provided for all their needs. Whenever the turned the captivity of His people and brought deliverance, the people freely gave to one another and to the poor. God has given us all things pertaining to life and death. *(Psalms 23:1; 18:34-36; II Peter 1:3)*

5. **God Divine Promotions**. Promotion comes from God. You never have to step on someone else to try to get ahead. When your time comes, nobody can stop God from blessing you. *(Psalms 102:13)*

6. **God's Protection:** God protects us from the blast of the evil one. Though a thousand fall at our side, and ten thousand at our right hand, He has not allowed it to come near us. *(Psalms 27:2, 34:7-9, 91; Isaiah 54:17)*

7. **Expected Outcome**: Only God can give us the outcome we desire. There is an end to our struggles, and we will not be disappointed. *(Psalms 30:5; Jeremiah 29:11; Proverbs 23:18)*

About the Author

Toni Wright is an author, gifted speaker, educator, mother, and grandmother. As an educator, she has influenced the lives of many young men and women. Toni has two Master of Education degrees, one in training and performance development and the other in organizational psychology. As a result of many trials and personal experiences, Toni understands that God controls the events in our lives and the world. For several years, Toni taught Bible studies, Sunday school classes, and women's groups. Toni's teaching experience allowed her to speak into the lives of numerous men and women from diverse backgrounds.

Toni believes that the Book of Esther serves as an excellent companion at this particular day and time because it speaks to the many explosive and chaotic events that people are dealing with today. While the circumstances may be slightly different, the behaviors, attitudes, and motivations behind the attacks from Satan are the same. The Book depicts racial injustice, hatred, wickedness in high places, murder, and men doing whatever they think is right in their hearts without regard to others. Judges 21:25. Nonetheless, the Book of Esther gives the people of God hope, inspiration, and victory. I hope that as you read this book, you will be motivated to keep fighting because you realize that as long as God is with you, the battle has already been won through Jesus Christ, our Lord.

The story is an excellent reminder of God's providence and His dealings with the people of God. It illustrates God's agape love for His people, His sobering patience, and care amid the many storms and challenges we face in life. Be encouraged.

Contact us at:
Higher Ground Daily Inspirations
www.grace2wright.org

Conclusion

Throughout the Bible, we see how God has intervened in the affairs of man. In the Book of Exodus, the 14th Chapter, the Bible tells us in verse 14 that, *"The LORD shall fight for you, and ye shall hold your peace."* As we study the Book of Esther, we learn that there are times when we should hold our peace, and there are times when we must take an active role in our fight against the enemy. We can be assured that God sees and knows everything that we go through, and He is in control of everything, regardless of how it looks.

"The LORD himself goes before you and will be with you; he will never leave you nor forsake you. Do not be afraid; do not be discouraged." Deuteronomy 31:8

Esther sought God's assistance before going into combat with the foe, and God was with her. She fasted and prayed to God for courage, knowledge, and favor, and she found God to be trustworthy. God brought Esther to the palace for such a time as this, and the Jews were delivered. *"And he changeth the times and the seasons: he removeth kings, and setteth up kings: he giveth wisdom unto the wise, and knowledge to them that know to understand." Daniel 2:21.*

Seven Things to Keep in Mind About the Book of Esther

8. <u>God's Providence:</u> Esther's life has been under God's watchful eye since the day she was born; in fact, the Bible says, "before the foundation of the world."

9. <u>Courage:</u> Courage can manifest itself in a variety of ways. Esther exhibited bravery in revealing her identity and her opponent to the king. Mordecai needed bravery to do the many things he did, adopting a little girl, exposing the King's assassination, and opposing evil Haman. And it took courage for Vashti to say "No" to the King, knowing that her reign as queen would come to an end.

10. <u>God's Mercy</u>: The Bible says that *"God is good! His mercy endures forever. Psalms 136:1.* And the one I love so much is *Lamentations 3:22-23 "It is of the Lord's mercies that we are not consumed because his compassions fail not."* He did not blame or judge Israel for their faults or how they came to be in their current situation. He was forgiving and merciful. Sometimes, people believe God may withhold deliverance because they did not do everything perfectly. However, God is gracious and compassionate toward both the just and the unjust.

11. <u>Jehovah-Jireh</u>, God supplies all our needs. God equipped the people of God with everything they needed to prevail in their conflict and beyond. They willingly gave to one another and the poor. Yet, they never confiscated their enemy's possessions for their own needs.

12. **God Divine Promotions**. You must resist the temptation to step on others to obtain a seat at the table. When the time is right for you, God has already made provision. *Psalms 102:13, "Thou shalt arise, and have mercy upon Zion: for the time to favor her, yea, the set time, is come."* God's timing is the best because He sees the big picture.

13. **God's Protection**: Numerous scriptures speak of God's security. Among my personal favorites is, *"When the wicked, even mine enemies and my foes, came upon me to eat up my flesh, they stumbled and fell." Psalms 27:2.*

14. **Expected Outcome**: Only God can give us the outcome that we desire. *Jeremiah 29:11 says, "For I know the thoughts that I think toward you, saith the LORD, thoughts of peace, and not of evil, to give you an expected end."*

    "For his anger endures but a moment; in his favor is life: weeping may endure for a night, but joy comes in the morning." Psalms 30:5.

Conversational Thoughts

- In the United States, there are over 248,000 underage marriages, with 80 percent of the girls marrying an adult. In the U.S. and across the world, child marriage and forced marriage disproportionately affect girls and women[4]."
- Vashti replied, "No." How critical is it to teach other women the value and strength of saying "no," even if they do not obtain their desired status? Numerous women have said "no" to unwelcome sexual advances, but you may not have heard about them because their perpetrators were never identified. Saying "no" is entirely up to you, just as it was for Vashti. Unfortunately, people still find themselves put in a position to choose to say "no" without repercussions.
- How would you explain Vashti's choice to your daughter or young people's Sunday School class studying the Book of Esther?
- How important is it for Christian women who hold leadership positions to be role models to other married women?

---

[4] https://www.unchainedatlast.org/child-marriage-shocking-statistics/

I HAVE GIVEN YOU THE POWER TO REWRITE YOUR FUTURE.

Esther kept pleading with the King to reverse wicked Haman's edict against the Jews until the King reminded her of what he had given her. The King reminded Esther that he could not undo something he had already signed and sealed with his ring. By giving Esther the house of Haman and giving Mordecai his ring, he conferred upon Esther the power to rewrite the Jews' future. This is the same ring he had given to Haman in Chapter 3. Now they had the power to rewrite the wrong that had been pronounced against them.

You may not be able to change your history or childhood, but God has empowered you to rewrite your future. Many individuals have scars from their past, but through the Holy Spirit and the power of His Name, you can still decide to be an overcomer. The negative decrees that have been spoken against your life by those used by Satan or the negative thoughts you tell yourself can be reversed by speaking God's saying what God says about you. God said you hold the power of *"life and death in your tongue."* Now, use it to rewrite your future. The King reminded them that whatever you write in my name with my seal cannot be reversed. (Esther 8)

Jesus said, "If ye shall ask anything in my name, I will do it." John 14:14

"His divine power has granted to us all things that pertain to life and godliness, through the knowledge of him who called us to his glory and excellence." 2 Peter 1:3.

Made in the USA
Middletown, DE
12 January 2022